Alphabetical Order

Michael Frayn was born in London in 1933 and read Russian, French and Moral Sciences (Philosophy) at Emmanuel College, Cambridge. He began his career as a journalist on the *Manchester Guardian* and the *Observer*. His award-winning plays include *Alphabetical Order*, *Make and Break* and *Noises Off*, all of which received Best Comedy of the Year awards, while *Benefactors* was named Best Play of the Year. Two of his more recent plays, *Copenhagen* and *Democracy*, also won numerous awards (including, for *Copenhagen*, the Tony in New York and the Prix Molière in Paris). In 2006 *Donkeys' Years* was revived in the West End thirty years after its premiere and was followed in 2007 by *The Crimson Hotel*, at the Donmar, and by *Afterlife*, at the National Theatre, in 2008. Frayn has translated Chekhov's last four plays, dramatised a selection of his one-act plays and short stories under the title *The Sneeze*, and adapted his first, untitled play, as *Wild Honey*. Frayn's novels include *Towards the End of the Morning* (in the USA, *Against Entropy*), *The Trick of It*, *A Landing on the Sun*, *Headlong* and *Spies*. His most recent books were a work of philosophy, *The Human Touch*, and *Stage Directions*, a collection of his writing on the theatre. He is married to the biographer and critic Claire Tomalin.

Michael Frayn

Alphabetical Order

Methuen Drama

Published by Methuen Drama 2009

1 3 5 7 9 10 8 6 4 2

Methuen Drama
A & C Black Publishers Limited
36 Soho Square
London W1D 3QY
www.methuendrama.com

First published in 1977 with *Donkeys' Years* by Eyre Methuen Ltd
Revised edition published by Methuen London Ltd in 1985
in *Frayn Plays: 1*
Revised for this edition 2009
Reprinted with changes to the text 2010

Copyright © 1977, 1985, 2009 by Michael Frayn

Michael Frayn has asserted his rights under the Copyright,
Designs and Patents Act 1988 to be identified
as the author of this work

ISBN: 978 1 408 12260 0

A CIP catalogue record for this book is available from the British Library

Typeset by Country Setting, Kingsdown, Kent

Alphabetical Order

Alphabetical Order was first presented at the Hampstead Theatre Club, London, by arrangement with Michael Codron on 11 March 1975, and it transferred to the Mayfair Theatre, London, on 8 April. The cast was as follows:

Lesley	Barbara Ferris
Geoffrey	A. J. Brown
Arnold	James Cossins
John	Dinsdale Landen
Lucy	Billie Whitelaw
Nora	June Ellis
Wally	Bernard Gallagher

Director Michael Rudman
Designer Alan Tagg

A version of this revised text was first presented at the Hampstead Theatre, London, on 16 April 2009. The cast was as follows:'

Lesley	Chloe Newsome
Geoffrey	Ian Talbot
Arnold	Gawn Grainger
John	Jonathan Guy Lewis
Lucy	Imogen Stubbs
Nora	Annette Badland
Wally	Michael Garner

Director Christopher Luscombe
Designer Janet Bird
Lighting Designer Tim Mitchell
Sound Designer Fergus O'Hare

Characters

Lesley
Geoffrey
Arnold
John
Lucy
Nora
Wally

Act One

The library of a provincial newspaper office.

The fabric of the building remains from the high tide of imperial and commercial confidence somewhere around the accession of George V. There are high wooden shelves around the walls containing standard works of reference, bound newspapers, unexplained brown envelopes and parcels and old milk bottles. Steel filing cabinets, chest high, are arranged in walks and alleys like a maze. In front of the cabinets are two work tables, pushed together to face each other, with three chairs. On the tables: a telephone, files of yellowing newspapers, folders, books.

Every surface in the room is occupied by yellowing cuttings, open telephone directories, and yesterday's evening papers. Some of the drawers of the filing cabinets are open, blocking the alleys. On one filing cabinet stands a box of empty jam jars; on another a broken chair.

Lesley *enters. She is in her mid-twenties – shy, clever, violent. She looks round the room uncertainly, then sits down at one of the tables and waits.*

Geoffrey *enters. He is a hurrying, deft, well-disposed man who is nearing retirement. He puts copies of various daily papers on the table.*

Geoffrey   Oh, she's not here. Never mind. She'll be here in a minute.

Lesley   Thank you.

Geoffrey   You know what they say – it's not much, but it's home. You can put your things on the window ledge, look. That's where she puts hers . . . That's right. That's the way. She won't be long. She'll explain everything to you. She sits there, so if you sit yourself down here you'll be all right, you'll be lovely.

Lesley   Thank you.

Geoffrey   I'll just move these things off. I'll put them here, look, if she wants them. No, you'll be all right in here. Everyone likes Lucy.

Lesley   Yes, I met her at the interview.

Geoffrey   I'm the Messenger. I'm in and out all the time. I mind everybody's business. Yours included. Anything you want to know about this office, ask me.

Lesley   Thank you.

Geoffrey   Have you ever worked in a newspaper library before?

Lesley   Not in a newspaper library, no.

Geoffrey   Madhouse! Never mind – you'll get used to it. One thing I'll tell you now. This is my one word of advice, so listen carefully. The facts of life. All right? Every Tuesday, not later than half past four, go and see Miss Fisher – that's down the corridor, through the Tube Room, where you found me today, and second door on your right – Miss Fisher – the name's up on the door – every Tuesday; and she'll give you a clean hand towel. All right?

Lesley   Thank you.

Geoffrey   *But* . . . but, but, *but*! Soap you'll need to buy yourself. Get yourself a plastic box in Woolworths – keep it in your drawer – no one'll take it – you'll be all right.

Lesley   Thank you.

Geoffrey   That's you all set up in life, then.

He goes out.

Lesley *gets up and walks slowly about the room, looking at everything. She turns over the pages of an ancient bound file of newspapers, then looks at her fingers and wipes the dust off. She walks slowly along one of the alleys of the maze, gently but automatically closing the open drawers as she goes. She sits down, not where she was sat by* **Geoffrey***, or the chair where 'she' sits, but in the third chair. Pause. Then she gets up and opens all the drawers again, exactly as they were. She sits, in the third chair.*

Arnold *enters. He is a large man in his fifties, who moves and thinks very slowly.*

Lesley *jumps up.* **Arnold** *stops at the sight of her.*

Arnold   Oh.

Lesley   I'm afraid she's not here yet.

Arnold   Ah.

Lesley   I don't think she'll be long. Could I help at all?

Arnold   Umm . . .

Lesley   I'm the new Assistant Librarian. I'm afraid I don't really know where anything is. I don't know how the Library's arranged . . . But perhaps I could . . . do something?

Arnold   Hm. Yes. Well . . .

He goes out. **Lesley** *sits.*

Arnold *re-enters.*

Lesley *jumps up.*

Arnold   Thanks.

He goes out.

Lesley *sits. The telephone rings. She looks at it, decides to answer it and gets to it just as it stops ringing.*

John *enters. He is a rumpled, mannered man with the accent and style of New College and All Souls. His connection with the world and people around him seems intermittent and haphazard.*

John   Someone, some spokesman on education, I assume in the Labour Party . . . only I somehow have a hunch that he *wasn't* in the Labour Party, that it was someone more surprising than that . . . or possibly not, possibly it was someone quite obvious . . . anyway, whoever it was, he *said* . . . or perhaps wrote, but I think said . . . about two years ago, but it may have been three or four, or further back still . . . *something* to the effect that even corporal punishment was better than selection, because selection something like made I think it was brothers and sisters . . . brothers and sisters came into it somewhere . . . and selection made them into, I don't know, enemies, or something equally undesirable.

Lesley   I'm afraid I've only just arrived . . .

John   It was reported somewhere, in something, about halfway down a right-hand page.

Lesley   I don't really know how the Library works.

John   Yes, but I just want to know who said it. And also when they said it . . . and where they said it . . . and what it was they said . . . and whether they said it at all or whether I've merely imagined it. I'm writing a leader on, obviously enough, education. If it helps to know that, which I suppose it probably doesn't.

Lesley   I think the Librarian should be here any moment now.

John   (*wandering among the filing cabinets, opening drawers and pulling out folders*)   Most probably she'll have it filed under whoever said it, which we don't know, or the occasion they said it on, which we don't know either. But she may have it under Education. Or Selection. Or Corporal Punishment. Or Punishment Corporal. Or Labour Party. Or Parties Labour. I like your pendant thing.

Lesley   Oh . . . Thank you.

John   I find silver far more deeply affecting than gold. I often think – and when anyone says they often think something it usually means they've just thought of it now – I often think that you could divide mankind into as it were silver people and as it were gold people. With gold I associate words like endomorphic, somatic, meridional, holistic. Silver I tend to locate in a cluster which contains ectomorphic, cerebral, nocturnal, analytic. Do you recognise anything about yourself in that list? Probably not. But then I suppose all systems of classification break down at some point, some sooner than others, as for instance this library, which must have broken down around the time of the Boer War. So you're as we say *joining the paper*?

Lesley   Yes.

John   What strange things young people get up to these days. I wonder if it was something that was said at a party conference. I think she's got old party conferences in one of those brown-paper parcel things up there.

Lesley   Shall I get them down?

She takes the third chair from the table across to the shelves, and climbs on it.

John (*searching in the filing cabinet*)   I'll try Education . . . Where are we? Edinburgh, Editors' Guild of, Edmonton . . . Libraries . . . *Libraries*! (*He takes the folder out.*)

Lesley   This one's World War II, Middle East . . . This one's Korea.

John   I love the little hollows in the back of your knees.

Lesley   Sorry?

John (*looking at the folder*)   In the National Library of Wales there are two million printed books, and three and a half million deeds and documents. In the National Library of Wales!

Arnold *enters.*

Arnold   Oh.

Lesley   She's still not here, I'm afraid. You're sure there's nothing *I* can do?

Arnold   Umm . . .

John   You could try getting off his chair.

Lesley   I'm terribly sorry.

She gets down.

This is your chair?

Arnold   Yes.

Lesley   I'm so sorry.

Arnold   Thanks.

He pulls the chair back to the work table, and sits down.

Lesley   I didn't realise there was anyone else who worked in here.

John   There isn't.

Lesley   I mean . . .

John   He doesn't.

Arnold *sits gazing into space.* **John** *searches, and sings to himself.*

John
A, B, C, D, E, F, G,
J, B, D, T, X, Y, Z,
H, I, J, K, H, I, J,
V, W, X, Y, Q . . .

Lesley (*indicating her original chair*)   Is it all right if I sit here?

Arnold   Yes.

Lesley *sits.*

John   You haven't just arrived in this town, have you?

Lesley   The day before yesterday.

John   Oh God, I suppose I'd better take you out tonight and show you where the only decent Indian restaurant is.

Lesley   Oh. Thank you. Only . . .

Lucy *enters. She is an easy-going, good-humoured woman whom everyone likes. She is wearing a slightly improbable coat, and carrying a shopping bag.*

Lesley *jumps up.*

John   Purely to save you from malnutrition or food poisoning. I'll come and collect you when you finish work this evening . . . (*To* **Lucy**.) Oh, hello. You didn't die in that mysterious accident in Argentina in 1946, then?

Lucy   Is this the invitation to the Indian restaurant? Already?

John   What do you mean, already? The courts presumed you dead about five years ago.

Lucy (*to* **Lesley**)   I'm sorry about this.

Lesley   No, no.

John   Spokesman on education. Labour Party. Said. Or wrote. Or sang. Or whistled . . .

Lucy   A quote?

John   Whacking kids better than selecting them.

Lucy   Hold on. (*To* **Lesley**.) They're all mad in this place. Aren't they, Arnold?

Arnold   Yes.

Lucy   What are *you* on today?

Arnold   Witches.

Lucy   Witches. I'll see what we've got. (*To* **Lesley**.) I suppose I should be making a speech of welcome, should I?

Lesley   Oh. No.

Lucy   I should be doing something. Telling you about the traditions of the paper, showing you where the loo is. I should have been here when you arrived, at any rate! God, that's awful, not even being here! It's not two o'clock yet, though, is it . . . ?

John   It *was* two o'clock, once upon a time.

Lucy   I'm so sorry! I've been standing dithering in the Oxfam shop for the last half-hour. (*Demonstrates the coat.*) Five quid. Yes? No?

Lesley   Great.

Lucy   Arnold?

Arnold   Um . . . ?

Lucy   Coat.

Arnold   Oh . . . (*Approves.*) Um.

Lucy   John? Any thoughts?

John   You know I hate thinking when I'm not on duty.

Lucy *takes the coat off and examines it.*

Lucy   I'm never going to wear it, am I . . . God, it's absolutely vile! File it with the jam jars . . . (*To* **Lesley**.) So! You're here! The great day at last! You're going to be such a help to me! You're going to transform this place!

John   Oh, please!

Lesley   I'm sure it doesn't need to be transformed . . .

Lucy   No, we're all counting on you. You're going to perform miracles.

Lesley   So what shall I do first?

John   How about raising the Editor from the dead?

Lucy   Could you start on the cutting?

Lesley   The cutting. Right.

Lucy   If we don't get the cutting finished by five, when the subs come in and things start warming up, we'll be in trouble. Right. Now. In this office we only cut the *Times*, the *Guardian*, and ourselves. Look, two copies of each. So you can cut the back and the front of each page. You're cutting this, say. (*She cuts.*) Power Pay Talks Breakthrough. Cut it nice and neatly so that it doesn't mess up the other stories around it. Now, stamp it. *Times* – *Guardian* – us. Make sure you've got today's date on it. Then underline the key word in the headline so we know where to file it. Power Pay Talks Breakthrough . . . Pay. No, Power. No, Pay.

Arnold   Talks.

John   Breakthrough.

Lucy   Power. No, Pay, Pay, Pay. Well, your guess is as good as mine.

The telephone rings.

But try to make it something we've got headings for already, or else we have to make out another folder, and if we get many more folders in this place we'll all go crazy. (*Into the telephone.*) Library. Hold on. (*To* **Lesley**.) Now, when you've stamped it and marked it, put it carefully to one side in some quiet place for filing . . . And if you can't find a quiet place on the table anywhere . . . or on top of the filing cabinets, say . . . my tip is to use the floor. I use the floor for cutting on, as a matter of fact. I use the floor for everything. The floor's always clear in the early part of the day, because the cleaners come in every morning, and they take everything off the floor and put it on the tables. All right? (*Into the telephone.*) Hello . . . ? Oh . . . (*They've given up. She puts the telephone down.*) One enquiry swiftly dealt with.

Lesley Do I cut everything?

Lucy Oh God, no! Be very selective!

Lesley So what do I select?

Lucy You select . . . the kind of thing that the kind of people who produce our kind of paper would want to know about to go on producing a paper of our kind. Have you ever seen the paper?

Lesley I started taking it when I heard I'd got the job.

Lucy Good God.

John That's what's wrong with this paper. It's produced by the kind of people who read it.

Lucy Well, then, you know what kind of thing we want. Don't bother with sport, or fashion, or by-elections.

Arnold Except local by-elections.

Lucy Except local by-elections. In general we don't want speculations, predictions and guesses which are going to be out of date by tomorrow.

John Unless they're speculations, predictions and guesses by public figures, which we can later hold against them.

Lucy What we want are facts. Facts and figures.

Arnold Anything in millions.

Lucy Yes, millions are good.

Arnold Or billions.

Lucy   No, not billions. When you get into billions it's all fancy stuff.

John   Anything about education, for me. Also anything about Southern Africa, China, the despoliation of national parks, the destruction of public transport, energy reserves, or monosodium glutamate.

Lucy   Anything about white bread, for Charles Harland.

John   Anything that can be used against religious programmes on television and dogs shitting on the pavement.

Lucy   No colour pieces. No think pieces.

John   Except by members of the staff.

Lucy   Except, of course, by Arnold and John. And they're filed under Arnold and John.

Lesley   I see.

Lucy   Just start at the top left-hand corner of each page, and run your eye down the columns.

John   Don't read.

Lucy   Never read.

John   Reading causes a variety of pathological anxiety states.

Lucy   Reading slows you down. Rail Peace Hopes. – No, no hopes or fears. Nuclear Energy: Fears Grow. – Yes. Well, it's nuclear. (*She marks it.*) Storms Hit North-East. – No, no weather. And they can all drop dead in the North-East for all we care here. Worst Month Ever for Trade Figures. – Yes. Because it's trade, and it's full of little m's meaning millions, and it's the worst ever. Princess Shaken in Fall. – No, we don't care about royalty . . . (*She reads, absorbed.*) They still haven't found that little boy.

John   You're reading.

Lucy   It's five days now.

John   You're reading.

Lucy   Yes, never read.

John   Never read.

Lesley   Shall I cut it?

Lucy   No. Well, you get the general principle?

Lesley   I think so.

John   The general principle on which this library is organised is her.

Lucy   And what I've tried to do, since Eric died and I became Librarian, is simply to continue as he would have wished.

Lesley   I see.

Lucy   That was a joke. As one glance round the room might have told you. All right, that's you fixed.

Lesley *sets to work.*

Lucy   Now, witches. Medieval witches? Modern witches?

Arnold   Oh . . .

Lucy   Modern, I should think. Yes? This *is* a newspaper, after all.

John   What about my quote?

Lucy *goes to her bag and takes out a parcel. She gives it to* **John**, *and then begins to search in the filing cabinets.*

John   What's this?

Lucy   Nothing. Don't open it now.

John *opens the parcel, to reveal two freshly laundered shirts.*

John   Shirts. *My* shirts?

Lucy   I thought you might want them.

John   Yes, but not *here*.

Lucy   So where?

John   Wherever.

Lucy   Where's wherever?

John   *I* don't know. Your place.

Lucy   My place?

John   For when I'm there.

Lucy   Which will be when?

John   I don't know. Whenever.

Lucy   So when's whenever?

John   When's whenever . . . ? That's a philosophically rather interesting question.

Lucy   Oh God! (*She returns to the desk with the folder. To* **Lesley**.) What?

Lesley   US Warned of Soviet Space Lead.

Lucy   Were you listening to all that?

Lesley   No, no. US Warned of Soviet Space Lead.

Lucy (*sighing*)   I suppose so.

Lesley   Space?

Lucy   US. Or Soviet Union. Or Space.

John   Two shirts still don't solve my problems with the first leader.

Lucy (*giving* **Arnold** *a folder*)   Occultism. Not much in it.

Arnold   They took Megan into hospital this morning.

Lucy (*sitting, and putting her hand on his arm*)   Oh, Arnold, why didn't you say before?

Arnold   Sent the ambulance.

Lucy   Oh, poor old Meg.

Arnold   I don't know. Change of scenery.

Lucy   Is this still the same business with her back?

Arnold   Seems to have spread into her stomach now.

Lucy   Oh, God. But what do they think it is?

Arnold   Husband trouble.

Lucy   Haven't they said?

Arnold   They're doing a few tests. Putting some tubes down her.

Lucy   Poor Meg!

Arnold   She'll be all right. Loves that kind of thing.

Lucy   What about you?

Arnold   Oh.

Lucy   You'll just go and sit in the George all evening, won't you?

Arnold   Yes.

Lucy   You'll have tubes down you before long.

Arnold   Pour the beer straight down.

Lucy   You will, you know.

Arnold   Plumb me into the barrel.

The telephone rings.

Lucy   You watch out. (*Into the telephone.*) Library . . .

John   By my calculation – the calculation I'm doing on the back of the Education (Nursery Schools) file to stop myself going mad with boredom while I wait for my quote – by my calculation – which is based on the very incomplete data I've so far turned up in the files – by my calculation the world contains somewhere around two hundred and twenty-five billion billion billion billion atoms. Is the Government, we wonder, fully aware of the magnitude of the problem?

Geoffrey *enters, with a bulging dispatch case.*

Geoffrey   Oh, she's here, then? She's finally arrived? You're being looked after?

Lesley   Yes, thank you.

Geoffrey   At long last, she says. You'll be all right now. Lucy'll take you under her wing.

He unloads wrapped magazines and postal packets.

Here you are. That is what you've all been waiting for. This'll put some fun back in your life.

Lucy (*on the telephone*)   Hold on. I'll see what we've got. (*She puts down the telephone, and goes to the filing cabinets.*) Oh God, it's Geoffrey.

Geoffrey   Here you are, Lucy. Grub up. Come and get it.

Lesley   Magazines?

Geoffrey   Magazines. Medical journals. Foreign publications. You name it.

Lesley   Do we have to cut these as well?

Lucy   I'll show you what we do with these.

As she speaks she hurls them one by one like mortar bombs in either the general direction of the waste-paper basket or the general direction of an out-basket by the door.

Tripe. Tripe. Tripe. Science corr. Charles Harland. Tripe. Editor's wife. Tripe. Tripe.

She goes back to the filing cabinets.

Geoffrey   Isn't she lovely? I told you, didn't I?

Lucy   Don't take any notice of Geoffrey.

Geoffrey   Everyone loves our Lucy. I was right, wasn't I?

Lesley   Yes.

Lucy   Geoffrey is a kind of endurance test we put all new members of staff through.

Geoffrey   No, seriously, though, isn't she a smasher?

Lucy   It's like having some huge dog licking your face and knocking everything over with its tail.

Geoffrey   She is, though, isn't she? Isn't she? Isn't she?

Lesley   Yes. Great.

Geoffrey (*to* **Arnold**)   Hello! You in here again?

Arnold   Know anything about witches?

Geoffrey (*to* **Lesley**)   This is our star turn. Arnold here. Never in the News Room. Always in the Library. I don't know whether it's warmer in here, or what. Or whether he's got his eye on our Lucy.

Lucy *returns to the table.*

Geoffrey   What do you think, Lucy?

Lucy   Down, Geoffrey, down! (*Into the telephone.*) He *does* have an E on the end, he *was* named by the Commission of Inquiry, and he's dead. (*She puts the telephone down. It rings.*) Library . . .

John   If someone doesn't find me this quote soon I'm going to start calculating the number of atoms in the universe.

Geoffrey   Oh Gawd, there's John, having a crafty smoke behind the filing cabinets. Great character, John. Professor or something at Oxford he was. One of those colleges there. All something. All Saints, was it, John? All Mod Con? But he had to leave because he knew it all already. That right, John?

John (*conversationally*)   Fuck off, Geoffrey.

Lucy   The new divorce law? I'll have a look. (*She goes to the filing cabinets.*)

Geoffrey   Oh, I pull their legs all right. Don't I, John?

John   You must have got a great pile of decomposing legs hidden away somewhere.

Geoffrey   No, seriously, though, in this office we really are just one great big happy family.

Lucy *hangs her tongue out and pants like a dog.*

Geoffrey   No, I'm being serious now.

John *barks.*

Geoffrey   I know that's often said.

Arnold *howls.*

Geoffrey   But in this case it's true. Isn't it, John? Bear me out on this.

John   It's a kind of basketwork group.

Geoffrey   That's right. We all help to keep each other sane.

Lucy   It's a madhouse, in other words. (*She howls.*)

John *barks.* **Arnold** *howls.*

Lucy (*into the telephone*)   There are an awful lot of divorce laws. Which one do you want . . . ? Children . . . ? What, here . . . ? No – adults, I'm afraid.

Geoffrey   I told you, didn't I? We all play the fool together.

John   It's a sheltered workshop. Well, we lose half a million pounds a year, and here we all are, unemployable but still employed.

Lucy (*into the telephone*)   Hold on. (*She crosses to the filing cabinets.*)

John   Are you looking for my quote?

Lucy   No.

Geoffrey (*to* **Lesley**)   This must all seem very strange to you, coming in from the outside. But we've got our own little ways of doing things here.

Lucy   It's a mess, in other words.

Geoffrey   Yes, but what a mess!

John   What a mess!

Lucy   What a mess!

Lucy (*into the telephone*)   All right. The Matrimonial Causes Act, 1967. Which bit do you want . . . ? Oh, Pat! I see! Why didn't you say so before?

Geoffrey   Oh dear. Pat Walker?

John   Alan off on his travels again?

Lucy   Don't cry, Pat, love. Just tell me.

John   Take her mind off it. Ask her who said that corporal punishment was better than selection.

Lucy (*into the telephone*)   I'm sorry, love, there are people shouting . . .

Geoffrey   They all come to Lucy! (*To* **Arnold**.) Now, what was *your* problem? Witches. (*To* **Lesley**.) You see? We all give each other a hand in this office. (*To* **Arnold**.) Witches. They think there's something in it now, don't they?

Arnold (*interested*)   Do they?

Geoffrey   Oh, they're very respectful about it now. There was this write-up about this doctor, and he said, frankly, all medicine was really witchcraft pure and simple. He said that when he wrote out a prescription for pills, it was no different from what they did in the old days when they recited a spell.

Arnold   Do Not Exceed the Stated Dose. You may turn into a frog.

Geoffrey   Well, it's all in the mind, isn't it? It's all up here.

Lucy (*into the telephone*)   Pat, I honestly can't see anything here about cruelty to domestic pets.

Geoffrey   Oh dear, Alan stepped on the cat on the way out.

John *makes a noise like a trodden cat.* **Arnold** *croaks.*

John   What?

Arnold *croaks.*

John   That's not a cat.

Arnold   Frog.

Lucy (*into the telephone*)   No. Arnold venturing one of his rare contributions to the conversation.

Arnold   So where was this article?

Geoffrey   *News of the World.*

Arnold *gets to his feet.*

Geoffrey   I'll do it. I'll find it. Don't move.

He crosses to the shelves where complete files of newspapers are kept and begins to pull them out and go through them. **Arnold** *subsides.*

Geoffrey   You don't want to go running all over the place and phoning people up if somebody's written it down for you already.

John   Arnold's a great believer in recycling.

Arnold   It may be raining outside.

Geoffrey (*to* **Lesley**)   No, what you have to remember is that this paper is unique. There's nothing like it anywhere else in the world.

John   There was, but it died in captivity.

Geoffrey   No, but it's true, isn't it?

Lucy (*into the telephone*)   Listen, love, I think what you ought to do is just frankly punch him in the eye . . . (*To the others.*) Oh. That wasn't what she wanted to hear at all. (*She puts the telephone down.*)

Geoffrey   No, but these things have got to be said. Somebody's got to tell Pat Walker to punch Alan in the eye. Somebody's got to tell this young lady what kind of organisation she's working for. Am I right, Lucy?

Lucy   No.

The telephone rings.

Library . . .

Geoffrey   No. There she goes. She's off. I told you, didn't I?

Lucy (*into the telephone*)   Hold on. (*She crosses to the files.*) Violence, Violence, Violence, Violence . . .

Nora *enters. She is an awkward-shaped woman in her fifties, and is carrying a stack of battered timetables.*

Nora (*singing*)   Happy birthday to you! Happy birthday to you! Happy birthday, dear Lucy . . .

Geoffrey   Oh, here she is. The lady herself.

Nora   Hello, Geoffrey.

Geoffrey   Hello, Nora.

Nora   Hello, John. Hello, Arnold . . . (*She sings to* **Lucy**, *dumping timetables.*) Happy birthday to you! And look – new shoes!

Lucy   Smashing.

Nora   I do feel a smart little girl.

Lucy   Lovely.

Nora   Last pair in the shop.

Lucy   Is that stuff for me?

Nora   I was clearing out my cupboards upstairs, and I thought, I know who'd like these.

Lucy   Old railway timetables?

Nora   Yes! 1950 to 1959. Somebody's going to be doing a piece about railways in the fifties, sooner or later. Isn't it nice when you think of just the right home for something?

Lucy   Wonderful. (*Into the telephone.*) 23,443. That's crimes of violence against the person.

Nora   Oh, I *am* pleased with my shoes! Isn't it lovely when you just get the last something in the shop? Or when you see exactly the right thing for what you want? They had a lovely round lace tablecloth in Swaddling's today, and I knew at once it was just right for the table in Mum's front room.

Lucy   Marvellous. (*Into the telephone.*) Sexual offences? Hold on. (*She crosses to the filing cabinets.*)

Nora   It's like putting the last piece in the jigsaw at Christmas. I get goose pimples all over and a little shiver inside me. I feel as if I'm snuggling down under the covers on a winter's night. (*To* **Lesley**.) You're the new girl in the school, aren't you? My name's Nora. I'm the Features Editor, for my sins. And what's your name?

Lesley   Lesley.

Nora   Lesley. That's a pretty name. I like that. I think it suits you. It's funny how some people's names are just right for them. Like Geoffrey. One look at him, and you can see he's a Geoffrey.

Geoffrey   What about Arnold, then?

Nora   Oh, Arnold's a real Arnold. Aren't you, Arnold?

Geoffrey   And John here.

Nora   Yes, John's a John all right, and Lucy's a Lucy.

Lesley   Can I help you at all?

Nora   Bless you, I just wanted to show off to Lucy in my lovely new shoes, because there's no fun in having lovely new shoes if you haven't got anyone to show them off to. I think you're going to enjoy working here. Lucy's such a sweet girl. Oh, we all love Lucy.

John   She knows. Geoffrey's told her.

Geoffrey   Never mind that. You tell her again.

Nora   Oh yes, we all dote on Lucy.

Lucy (*into the telephone*)   Right, sexual offences . . .

Nora   She's done wonders in here since poor Eric died. I believe you're going to fit in here very snugly. Because I have a funny feeling that you're our sort of person.

Lucy (*into the telephone*)   6,656. Do you want that broken down into rape, sodomy, bestiality, and so on?

Nora   Bless her heart! No, we all dote on Lucy. Don't we, Arnold? And of course we're all very fond of Arnold. Aren't we, Arnold? Oh, we'd all be very sad if Arnold ever had to leave us. Even though he is rather a bad boy from time to time. But he's making great efforts to be good these days, and we're all very proud of him. And he writes like an angel. What are you working on today, Arnold?

Arnold Shipbuilding.

Nora Well, I look forward to reading that. Arnold dear, how is Megan?

Arnold Fine.

Lucy (*hand over the telephone*) She went into hospital this morning.

Nora Oh, Arnold. I *am* sorry. What's the trouble?

Arnold Greenfly.

Nora (*to* **Lesley**) Arnold has a lovely wayward humour which we all greatly treasure. (*To* **Arnold**.) Nothing serious, I hope?

Arnold They're spraying her.

Nora It's not her back again?

Arnold Four times a day after meals.

Nora (*reproachfully*) Arnold!

Arnold Caution: Do Not Exceed the Stated Dose.

Geoffrey He's off.

Arnold Put that spray gun down, Nurse!

Nora (*to* **Lesley**) He's great fun, when you get used to him.

Arnold Too late! (*He croaks.*)

Nora And then there's John. You've met John?

Lesley Yes.

Nora John's another much-loved character. Aren't you, John . . . ? But answer came there none. Well, that's John.

And Geoffrey you must have met when you arrived. Whatever should we do without Geoffrey?

Geoffrey   You'd all be sunk, wouldn't you?

Nora   It's really Geoffrey who runs the whole paper, I do firmly believe.

Geoffrey   Nora's the one. Gives us all a pat on the back each day.

Nora   Thank you, Geoffrey.

Geoffrey   Any time, Nora.

Nora   No, I appreciate that. Because I do think that someone ought to tell people they're loved and needed.

Arnold *croaks.*

Geoffrey   No, that's right. You tell them, Nora.

Nora   Yes, I will. And it's jolly nice to be told it back once in a while.

Wally *enters. He is a trimly moustached, brisk, waggish man in his forties.*

Wally   Lucy, my love! Are you ready?

Geoffrey   Oh Gawd, it's Wally!

Nora   Hello, Wally!

Geoffrey   Now the party's all complete.

Nora   How's Wally today?

Wally *pays no attention to anyone except* **Lucy***. He embraces her and kisses her non-telephone ear.*

Wally   Are you packed? What have you done with your suitcase?

Lucy (*into the telephone*)   Sharp instrument – 53. Blunt instrument – 26.

Wally (*to* **Lesley**)   What's this – the football results?

Lucy (*into the telephone*)   Hitting, kicking, etc. – 10.

Nora   Wally, this is Lesley. She's the new girl in the class. A great joker is Wally.

Geoffrey   Yes. Take no notice of Wally.

Wally (*to* **Lesley**)   Lucy and I are secretly running off together. Not a word!

Lucy (*into the telephone*)   Strangulation or asphyxiation – 28.

Wally   As soon as she's finished on the phone, we're away.

Lucy (*into the telephone*)   Shooting – 16. Other methods – 5.

Wally (*to* **Lucy**)   If that's the milkman, tell him to start the milk again on Monday week.

Lucy (*into the telephone*)   All right . . . ? Don't mention it. Bye. (*She puts the telephone down.*) Hello, Wally. What do *you* want?

Wally   We're off.

Lucy   Today's the day?

Wally   Today's the day, as ever was.

Lucy   You've got the tickets?

Wally   The carriage awaits.

Lucy   We're going by carriage?

Wally   I've got the tickets.

Lucy   Then off we go.

Wally   Off we go! – Oh . . . just one thing. USDAW.

Lucy (*going to the filing cabinets*)   USDAW.

Wally   Must just look at the cuttings on the Union of Shop, Distributive and Allied Workers, and write a little piece about the strike. Then we're away.

Lucy   Then we're away.

Nora   I do hope you're not giving Lesley the wrong impression.

Wally (*indicating* **Lesley**)   Is she coming, too?

Geoffrey   Oh Gawd!

Nora   How are Jane and the children?

Wally   *And* you?

Nora   Jane and the children – how are they?

Wally   By all means. Be my guest. What about Geoffrey?

Geoffrey   Never stops, does he? What a man!

Nora   Four lovely children.

Wally   The USDAW file. That's all that's holding us up.

Lucy   I've seen it somewhere.

Wally   Can't find it?

Lucy   I had it in my hands last night.

Wally   Under the clean shirts?

Geoffrey   Terry Lapping's got it. Or Charles Harland.

Wally   In the larder? (*Searches.*) Under the sideboard?

Lucy   It's in here somewhere.

Geoffrey   It'll be in the subs.

Lucy   I remember distinctly, I put it *here*.

Nora   Come on, chaps. The search parties are out.

Geoffrey   It'll be under all these papers somewhere. USDAW?

Nora   USDAW.

Lesley   It's not one of those folders on the shelf up there?

Lucy   Then I cleared everything off here, and put it over here. No, here.

Wally   It'll be in that box with the wellies in the hall.

Nora   It couldn't have fallen into the waste-paper basket, could it?

Lucy   Then I put all the stuff on here on the floor.

Geoffrey   This is as good as a party!

Nora   Isn't it fun? I hope we all get choccy bickies for prizes.

Arnold (*searches*)   What are we looking for?

Lesley   USDAW.

Arnold (*baffled*)   USDAW?

Wally   I've found two lumps of sugar and a rubber mouse.

Lucy   The cleaners would have picked it up off the floor and put it probably here . . .

Geoffrey   I don't know what Lesley's going to make of it all. Look at her! She thinks we're all crackers!

Lesley   No, no.

Nora   No, she understands all right. Don't you, Lesley?

Geoffrey   It isn't always like this, you know.

John   No, sometimes we have bad days.

Nora   Dear old John, always looking on the gloomy side.

Wally   Oh, but she keeps a lovely house. You've got to give her that.

Lucy   Look, I could find this thing in two seconds if people didn't keep shifting everything round!

John   Oh dear, we're spoiling her system.

Lucy   What happened to all the stuff that was on here?

Geoffrey   I put it here.

Lucy   Then where is it now?

Nora   I think those are the things I shifted here.

Lucy   And here it is! Exactly where I put it!

Nora   That's not USDAW.

Geoffrey   That's UNRRA.

Lucy   Yes, because some fool's put it in the wrong folder! I remember now – I got it out to change it.

John   Oh dear.

Geoffrey   Anyway, she's found it.

Nora   Well done, Lucy.

Geoffrey   Lucy to the rescue, once again.

Lucy (*giving the folder to* **Wally**)   That's *you* fixed, then.

Wally   UNRRA?

Nora   On the cover.

Geoffrey   Inside – USDAW.

Wally   Oh, that's ingenious.

Nora   All's well that ends well.

John   That's the way we do things in this office.

Geoffrey   That's us.

John   Cry God for Lucy, England and Saint Jude. Saint Jude being the patron saint of lost causes.

Nora   Well, I'm sorry if I sound old-fashioned, but I do think we've got to give ourselves credit where credit is due. After all, we've jolly well got our backs to the wall. If we don't believe in ourselves, who else is going to believe in us?

Silence.

Wally   Is it Armistice Day?

Arnold *walks heavily out.*

Geoffrey   Oh, he's off.

John   Couldn't stand the emotional strain.

Nora   Poor old Arnold. How's he going to manage while Megan's in hospital?

Lucy   Live in the George, I suppose.

Nora   Someone ought to see he gets an evening meal.

Lucy   Someone ought.

Nora   Well . . . I must go and show Esther Edwards my new shoeses. Make her jealous. (*To* **Lesley**.) Now, you are going to look after our Lucy, aren't you? Because she's our very own and special Lucy, and couldn't ever be replaced.

Lesley *nods and smiles.*

Nora   There's a good girl.

She goes out.

Geoffrey   Poor old Nora.

Lucy   Poor old Nora.

Geoffrey   You know where's she's off to, don't you?

Lucy   I can guess.

Geoffrey   Chasing after Arnold. Get him on supper parade tonight.

Lucy   Poor old Arnold.

Geoffrey   She'll get him in the end, you know. Six to four on. I'd better go and rescue him. I'll take him his write-up in the *News of the World*. Don't do anything I wouldn't.

He goes out.

John   Poor old Geoffrey.

Lucy   Why poor old Geoffrey?

John   Why not poor old Geoffrey? What's Geoffrey done that he shouldn't be poor old Geoffrey, like everybody else? Oh God. Nearly time for the first tea trolley. Look, will you phone me with that quote? And don't forget to say 'poor old John' as soon as I'm out of the room.

He goes out. Silence. He comes back.

Come on – 'Poor old John'. I'm waiting behind the door to hear it.

Lucy   You won't hear anything by hanging about behind the door.

John   No, I sometimes suspect I've so little objective reality that people don't even talk about me behind my back.

He goes out.

Wally   Poor old John.

Lucy   Off you go, then, Wally. You've got your folder.

Wally *looks down at the folder.* **Lucy** *smiles.*

Lucy   We'll run away together another time.

Wally *smiles.*

Lucy   One of these days. Yes?

Wally *looks at her.* **Lucy** *looks at him, and then away at* **Lesley**.

Wally (*to* **Lesley**)   Take care of her then. Don't lose her. I'm putting you in charge of her.

He goes out. Silence. **Lesley** *works.*

Lucy   Well, what do you think?

Lesley   Scientists Warn of Danger in Turnips?

Lucy   Yes. Anything scientific. What do you think of them all?

Lesley   He's deaf, isn't he?

Lucy   Deaf? Who – Wally?

Lesley   The one who wanted the USDAW file.

Lucy   Wally's not deaf.

Lesley   Oh. I thought that was perhaps why he kept making all those jokes.

Lucy   That's just Wally. That's just the way he is.

Lesley   I thought perhaps it was so he didn't have to hear what people said to him.

Lucy   He's not deaf. Well . . . Not *deaf.*

She sits down at the table and begins to cut.

I'm sorry about Arnold. He seems to have moved in here
permanently. I don't know quite how that happened. He's
mad, of course.

Lesley   His wife's ill?

Lucy   I don't suppose it's anything serious.

Lesley   I gather from what he was saying that he doesn't get
on with her.

Lucy   He gets on with her.

Lesley   Oh. I thought from what he was saying . . .

Lucy   He gets on with her all right. Anyway, who gets on
with their wife?

Lesley   I just thought perhaps that's why he drank. Liberals
Quietly Confident at Dunfermline?

Lucy   Look, Arnold's all right.

Lesley   Yes, I liked him.

Lucy   We're all on Arnold's side.

Lesley   He seems very nice.

Lucy   I don't know whether it helps, going round sticking
labels on people.

Lesley   I'm sorry. It was just something that woman with
the glasses said.

Lucy   Nora? Oh, Nora. What did you make of her?

Lesley   I thought she seemed . . . very nice.

Lucy   She's all right. Well, Arnold can't stand her. That's the
only thing. We all have to protect Arnold from her. Actually,
John can't stand her, either. Nor can I, now I come to think
about it . . . I suppose she's all right apart from that. Oh God,
John's quote.

Lesley   Liberals Quietly Confident at Dunfermline?

Lucy   John and I are living together, incidentally. I'd better tell you that before you make any remarks about *him*. Well, on and off. *Were* living together.

Lesley   Liberals Quietly Confident at Dunfermline?

Lucy   Or still are, even. Who knows? No. No by-elections. (*She watches* **Lesley**.) Oh dear. You're not very impressed with us, are you?

Lesley   Impressed?

Lucy   You're supposed to be overawed, coming to work here.

Lesley   It's all very interesting.

Lucy   But you're not *overawed* exactly.

Lesley   Overawed?

Lucy   You don't see a kind of . . . halo round everything?

Lesley   A halo?

Lucy   A kind of glow that makes sense of everything.

Lesley (*looking round the room*)   Well . . .

Lucy   You don't.

Lesley   A glow?

Lucy   A kind of excitement, a kind of desirability.

Lesley   Things don't glow.

Lucy   Of course not.

Lesley   I mean, they don't give off excitement. The excitement's in you, not in the things. Things aren't exciting in themselves. Are they? It's just what we do with them, what use we make of them. *I* think. Isn't it?

Lucy   Yes.

Lesley   Sorry.

Lucy   No, you're right.

Lesley   Church Report Finds Spectre of Alcoholism Over the Vicarage?

Lucy   Yes. Anything religious. *I* was overawed, when I first came here. I suppose things were different then. Oh, I don't know. That chair was up there. I must admit the jam jars weren't. But everything people said seemed to be funny. I just laughed and laughed. I did nothing but laugh for about three years. All I can remember doing is standing in the George in the middle of the day, drinking Draught Guinness, surrounded by very tall men who gazed slowly down into their beer and then said things that made me laugh.

Lesley   That was Arnold, was it?

Lucy   I didn't see you doing much laughing.

Lesley   When?

Lucy   When they were all in here.

Lesley   They weren't saying things to make people laugh.

Lucy   Weren't saying things to make people laugh? What do you mean? We were all performing away like lunatics!

Lesley   Performing?

Lucy   For you!

Lesley   Oh. I see.

Lucy   Good God, you don't think we're that lovable normally?

Lesley   Lovable?

Lucy   Oh. You didn't think we were that lovable even then.

Lesley   Family Die on M1?

Lucy   How many?

Lesley   Four.

Lucy   No. Funny, really. There was this whole venerable organisation clowning away for an audience of one. And there was the audience gazing coldly back.

Lesley Not coldly.

Lucy Not warmly.

Lesley Not coldly or warmly.

Lucy Objectively.

Lesley Isn't that right?

Lucy Fine. Unless you happen to be the object.

Lesley I'm sorry.

Lucy Classifying away. This is a deaf man. This is a drunk.

Lesley I didn't say that.

Lucy No. You saw it.

Lesley I didn't see it like that.

Lucy You looked.

Lesley I couldn't not look.

Lucy You looked, and I saw.

Arnold *enters. He walks slowly back to his place at the table, sits down, and gazes into space.* **Lucy** *watches him.*

Lucy I suppose we're done for, really. If you look at it objectively. Not much future for local institutions. Everything has to be centralised these days.

Lesley That depends.

Lucy What, on us?

Lesley Don't you think?

Lucy On me? On Arnold?

Lesley Well, on me, too.

Lucy You're a great believer in local institutions, are you?

Lesley Aren't you?

Lucy Why aren't you more impressed with this one, then?

Lesley   You mustn't let yourself be impressed by something you believe in. That's what's wrong with this place.

The telephone rings.

Lucy (*into the telephone*)   Library . . . Oh, hello. How are you . . . ? Are you? That's nice . . . Hold on, I'll just look.

She puts her hand over the telephone, and searches in the paper she is cutting.

The Vice Chancellor's wife. God, I hate this town! (*Into the telephone.*) Seven fifteen. But the main film doesn't begin until eight fifty-three . . . Of course not. Any time. Enjoy yourselves. (*She puts the telephone down.*) I'm not really cut out for this sort of work. Actually, that's quite funny.

Lesley   Yes.

Lucy   Laugh then.

Lesley *smiles.*

Lucy   Or perhaps I've been cut out for it, but I haven't been marked up. I don't know which folder I'm supposed to be in. That's another joke . . . Do *you* feel like a librarian?

Lesley   Among other things.

Lucy   What other things?

Lesley   Various other things.

Lucy (*to* **Arnold**)   She wants to be a reporter.

Arnold   Probably.

Lucy   She's hoping the News Editor will notice her. Big fire one afternoon in the city centre, and all the reporters out on jobs.

Arnold   Except me.

Lucy   Except you. (*To* **Lesley**.) *Are* you hoping to move on to higher things?

Lesley   Britain Sicily of Europe by 1980, Warns Car Chief?

Lucy   No. No warnings, except from scientists. So *are* you?

Lesley   Sometime. Not yet.

Lucy   I'm counting on you to help me get this place straight first.

Lesley   Yes, of course.

Lucy   I mean I really am. We all are. We're in a mess. I think *I'm* coming to pieces, for a start. I mean literally! Everything inside my head is coming unstuck. I was trying to get to sleep the other night when I suddenly realised I didn't know who Catherine of Braganza was. I knew I'd known. I knew I knew the name. I knew she fitted into something somewhere. But was it the Dissolution of the Monasteries or was it the War of the Spanish Succession? And then I realised I didn't know where the War of the Spanish Succession fitted in. Was it something to do with the Holy Roman Empire? Or did it somehow come into Pitt's First Ministry? Catherine of Braganza . . . I knew the name as well as I knew the name Catherine Porter.

Lesley   Catherine Porter?

Lucy   Catherine Porter used to sit next to the radiator, between Valerie Wells and Sally Grant. At least, she did when we were in the Remove. Where did she sit when we were in 5A? Was it by the art cupboard, between Sandra Lewis and Rosemary Levenson . . . ? Oh God – I can't remember *that* now!

Lesley   I thought Catherine of Braganza was Charles the Second's wife?

Lucy   Oh. Thanks.

Lesley   Sorry.

Lucy   No. Nice to know.

Silence.

Lesley   How old is Wally?

Lucy   Forty-nine.

Lesley   How old are you?

Lucy   Why?

Lesley   Because I don't see what you're waiting for.

Arnold *starts writing.*

Lucy   You've given Arnold a shock, anyway. He's started his piece.

Lesley   Sorry. I shouldn't have said that.

Lucy   You're twenty-five.

Lesley   Yes.

Lucy   Well, you wouldn't see, would you?

Lesley   I suppose not.

Nora *enters.*

Nora (*to* **Arnold**)   Oh, you're back here. I've been looking for you everywhere. (*To* **Lucy**.) Just something I wanted to say to Arnold. Arnold dear, if you've got to go to the hospital, come round and have something to eat afterwards. In fact, I'll drive you there in my trusty Mini. How about that?

Arnold   Got to do something after the hospital.

Nora   What have you got to do, Arnold?

Arnold   Got to go somewhere.

Nora   Where have you got to go?

Arnold   Somewhere.

Nora   Arnold, it would be a dreadful pity if you started being a naughty boy again while Megan's not well.

Lucy   Nora . . .

Nora   I'm just trying to keep him out of mischief while Megan's away.

Lucy   But if he's got to go somewhere . . .

Nora He *says* he's got to go somewhere.

Lucy Well, if he *says* he's got to go somewhere . . .

Nora But I think he's fibbing. Aren't you, Arnold?

Pause.

Lucy He's having supper with me.

Nora Having supper with you? When was this arranged?

John *enters.*

John Somebody, some spokesman on education, and I have made the suggestion that he should be sought within the ranks of the Labour Party . . .

Lucy (*head in hands*) I know, I know. I haven't forgotten.

John Then what, as one might reasonably enquire, is the answer?

Lesley *goes quietly to the reference books and starts searching.*

Nora Lucy, darling, I don't want to go putting my foot in it, but won't you and John be wanting to have a quiet meal on your own together?

John Could we just get this quote sorted out? I have got two other leaders to write before edition time.

Lucy *sits, inert.*

Geoffrey *enters, with evening papers.*

Geoffrey What? No one got any work to do? What a good thing I called! Here you are – the evening papers. Top Civil Servant Vanishes. Rail Fares Up. Blonde Had Gelignite in Undies. In the shops – fivepence. To you – nothing.

He dumps the papers in front of **Lucy**.

Geoffrey What's the matter with Lucy?

Nora I think she's trying to do too much.

John I think she's trying to do too little.

Geoffrey   Come on, Lucy, cheer up. You'll be all right.
You've got Lesley to help you now. You've got John and Nora
and Arnold to keep you company.

Wally *enters.*

Geoffrey   You've even got Wally.

Wally   And this time we're definitely leaving!

Lucy *(lacklustre)*   What do you want now, Wally?

Wally   I've got a ladder outside the window.

Geoffrey   That's right, Wally. You cheer her up.

Wally   Where's the horse?

Lucy   He can't hear you.

Wally   The horse is holding the ladder. Right? Right! Off
we go. Oh – just one thing.

*He whips away the handkerchief he is holding, and reveals that the hand
is injured.*

Lucy   Oh my God! What happened?

Wally   Where do you want me to bleed? Over the *Times* or
the *Guardian*?

Lucy   Hold on. I'll get the first-aid box.

Geoffrey   Lucy'll soon have that bandaged up for you.

Nora   Have you washed it?

Wally   I don't know. I was just quietly putting my hand into
this jeweller's window . . .

Nora   Washed it. Have you washed it?

Wally   Actually I was just quietly punching the Editor on
the nose . . .

Geoffrey   Here she comes, the Lady with the Lamp.

John   A miracle she hasn't lost the first-aid box.

Lucy   But . . . the key . . .

John   And she's lost the key!

Nora   Oh dear. Lucy.

Lucy, **Geoffrey**, **John**, **Nora** *and* **Arnold** *all search urgently.* **Wally** *waits patiently.* **Lesley** *watches them all.*

Lucy   Everyone was helping themselves.

John   She's locked the first-aid box, and she's lost the key!

Lucy   It was my one bit of efficiency.

Nora   Oh dear, this could be rather serious.

Wally   Would you like me to die in here, or shall I go outside?

John (*to the world at large*)   We've got the box. But we can't open it.

Nora   This really is one of our less appealing muddles.

Lucy   Well, you look after it! I don't want to do it!

Geoffrey   Now let's all keep calm.

Lucy   I always get landed with these rotten jobs that no one else wants!

John   Hadn't we better discuss the injustice of the world later?

Lucy   Do the collections for farewell presents. Run the Christmas raffle.

Geoffrey   Come on, Lucy, love . . .

Lucy   Sell the tickets for the staff dance. Help with the children's treat . . . And I haven't got any children! I hate children!

Nora   No, you don't . . .

Lucy   Yes, I do! I hate their parents, too! And I'm sick of being nice! Everyone takes it for granted I'm nice, and I'm not, and I'm fed up with pretending to be! I'm also fed up with the effort of thinking everyone else is nice! I'm worn out with the sheer hard labour of seeing any sense in anything!

John   Sit down.

Geoffrey   Take a deep breath.

Lucy   I sit here all day keeping nothingness stuck together by sheer effort of will. And what happens? I lose the only thing that really matters! Now I have to watch Wally stand there and bleed to death!

John   He's not bleeding to death.

Wally   It is, you know. It's running up my sleeve.

Lucy   I'm sorry, Wally! I'm sorry! I've come all to pieces! I don't know what I'm doing!

Lesley *comes forward holding the leg of the broken chair, and opens the first-aid box with a single sharp blow. Silence.*

Geoffrey   Well, that's one way of doing it.

Lesley   Sorry. I thought probably we'd better not wait for the key. Sorry.

Lucy *dresses* **Wally**'s *hand.*

Nora   No. Well done.

Wally   Grand little helper you've got yourself here, Lucy.

John   What one might call a radical solution.

Wally   No, I'll tell you what I did. I spiked myself. Put myself on the spike. Threw myself away with the old copy. Psychosomatic self-crucifixion. Sad story.

Geoffrey   Anyway, you're all right now. What about you, Lucy? You back to earth again?

Lucy   I'm back to earth again.

Geoffrey   Because we don't care about old Wally bleeding to death. But we don't like to see you upset.

Nora   I think Lesley's cured two birds with one stone.

Geoffrey   Well, good for her!

Nora   Go to the top of the class!

Lesley *retires, embarrassed, to the book she was consulting earlier.*

Lesley   Anyway . . . 'A child is afraid of being whipped, and gets his task, and there's an end on't; whereas by exciting emulation and comparison of superiority, you lay the foundation of lasting mischief; you make brothers and sisters hate each other.'

John   Good God.

Lesley   Is that it?

John   Yes.

Lesley   Dr Johnson.

John   Dr Johnson? Oh, well, that's no use, then.

He turns to go.

Curtain.

Act Two

The same. But it has been transformed. All the clutter and rubbish in the room have disappeared, except on one of the two work-tables, which remains as chaotic as before. The tables have been separated, though, and moved to either side of the room, so that their occupants would now sit back to back. A small third table has been introduced in some inconspicuous corner, and a chair set at it with its back upon the room. There is a wire basket by the door, with an arrow pointing to it and a notice saying: 'Returned folders here.' On one wall is a typed notice with the heading: 'Please observe these simple rules.' On another wall: 'All folders must be signed for.' On the door: 'Have you signed for your folder?'

There is a single loose cutting on the floor. The telephone is ringing.

Lesley *enters. She goes to the work table with the telephone, automatically picking up the one misplaced cutting on the way, and puts down her briefcase. She takes off her coat and hangs it up. She returns to her desk, but instead of answering the telephone puts her briefcase away. She goes round the room, automatically shifting an odd misplaced volume back on to the shelves, straightening the chairs at the third table, etc. She contemplates the chaotic work-table, makes a move to tidy something on it, but then puts it back.*

The telephone stops ringing.

John *enters. He sprawls against a filing cabinet and thinks, without looking at* **Lesley**.

Lesley *glances at him, then goes to the 'Returned Folders' basket and takes out the folders in it. She checks them off in the signing-out book, then moves briskly about the filing cabinets, redistributing the folders to their proper places in the system.*

John   No, I think all I'm saying is this: does one want to be quite so as it were pigeonholed?

The telephone rings. **Lesley** *works on.*

John   Is that thing trying to tell us something?

Lesley   Not two o'clock yet. They know the rules.

She finishes replacing the folders, and takes another half-dozen folders out. The telephone stops ringing. She begins to work through one of the folders she has taken out, removing various cuttings from it and putting them aside.

John   I'm not saying one doesn't. Perhaps one does. I'm merely being a channel through which an unasked question can get itself asked.

No response.

Because one would be making a fairly definite statement about oneself. Would we be as the phrase goes happy about saying, 'We live in a converted stable block'? Imagine some other couple saying it. Some couple at a party. Glasses of white wine in hand. 'We live in a converted stable block.' How would we feel about them? I mean, I liked it as a place. I liked the little cobbled yard. I liked the pots of geraniums. I didn't much like the dustbins. No, I did quite like the dustbins. In a way I liked the dustbins more than the geraniums. I thought the dustbins left more as it were scope for the imagination. But the whole place does shout 'Nice young A/B couple with books and no money.' Doesn't it? 'He a leader writer, she a librarian. He refusing to move to a suburban semi, she refusing to live any longer in a conveniently situated flat in the centre just because people pee in the doorway.' Don't you think? Honestly?

No response.

I suppose what I'm really saying is that if one's going to state quite so definitely what sort of person one is, then one ought perhaps just to pause for a moment and make sure in one's own mind that one really is that sort of person.

Lesley   If we don't make up our minds today the place will be gone.

John   I'm just trying to imagine watering the geraniums.

Lesley   All right, we'll forget it.

John   No, if you think we should think about it, let's think about it.

Lesley   I don't think we should think about it, because if we think about it it'll be too late.

John   So what are you proposing?

Lesley   I think we should take it.

John   All right, let's think about taking it.

Lesley   But I don't think we should think about taking it if *you* don't think we should.

John   I do think we should.

Lesley   Take it?

John   Think about it.

Lesley   Look, we must get this straight. Are we trying to find a place or aren't we?

John   We are trying to find a place.

Lesley   That's settled?

John   That's settled.

Lesley   That's all I want to know.

John   Well, it *is* settled, isn't it?

Lesley   What do you mean, 'isn't it'?

John   I mean, so far as I know, it is.

Lesley   Here we go again. *So far as you know*, it's settled?

John   In so far as I am, in saying 'it's settled', not reporting upon the existence of a settlement, but committing myself to that settlement, it is, by my very act of saying 'it's settled', undoubtedly settled; but in so far as 'it's settled' is not the enactment of a settlement, but merely a report upon the existence of a settlement, then I can't report at first hand upon *your* adherence to the settlement, only my own. Which I do, though why we can't just go on living at your place I still don't see.

Lucy *enters in haste, wearing the Oxfam coat and clutching a supermarket carrier bag full of groceries.*

Lucy   Sorry. There was only one checkout working. Hello, John. Sorry, Lesley.

Lesley   It's only just after two.

Lucy *dumps the groceries on the confusion-covered desk.*

Lucy   I couldn't shop this morning because I was listening out for the baby downstairs.

Lesley   Don't worry about it!

Lucy   If she takes the baby she has to take the pram, and if she takes the pram she can't get on the bus, and if she can't get on the bus she arrives too late for the doctor to see the baby. Of course, if she leaves the baby at home the doctor doesn't see him either, but at least she has time to do some shopping.

She dumps her coat on top of the groceries.

Lesley   Wouldn't you be happier if we hung that up?

Lucy   Oh, sorry.

She picks it up, but **Lesley** *politely takes it and hangs it up for her.*

Lucy   Sorry.

She catches **John***'s eye and makes a pantomime of being put down.* **John** *wags his finger at her.*

Lesley (*turning*)   What?

John   What?

Lesley   I thought you made some sign.

John   No.

Lucy   What do you want me to do today?

Lesley   What do *you* think we should be doing?

Lucy   I hope you're just about to tell me.

Lesley   I was wondering if you might like to get on with marking up and cutting.

Lucy   Sure.

Lesley   Because I was wondering if you might like me to do some more discarding.

Lucy   Anything you say.

Lesley   We've still got a lot of dead wood to get rid of.

Lucy   Right. Where are the papers?

Lesley   I was wondering, do you think it would be a good idea if I got started on the old Balance of Payments folders?

Lucy   You've got started on them.

Lesley   Just while I was waiting.

Lucy   I *am* late.

Lesley   I was early.

Lucy   Sorry, anyway.

The telephone rings. **Lesley** *looks at her watch, then picks up the telephone.*

Lesley (*into the telephone*)   Library . . .

Lucy   My assistant is looking after you, is she? Nothing I can get you? A few cuttings? A cup of tea?

John   No, I'm just . . . you know . . .

Lesley (*into the telephone*)   Hold on for one moment. (*She goes to the filing cabinets.*)

Lucy   Just, you know. Of course. Sorry.

Lesley   Sorry?

Lucy   Sorry, I thought John was waiting for something.

Lesley   No, no. (*To* **John**.) We'll talk about it later. (*To* **Lucy**.) Sorry. (*To* **John**.) Go on, then.

John   Am I being tidied away?

Lesley   It's after two.

John   After two. Oh yes. After two. Sorry.

He goes out.

Lucy   Sorry. I didn't mean to break anything up.

Lesley   You weren't breaking anything up.

She goes back to the telephone with a folder of cuttings.

(*Into the telephone.*) In gross tons or short tons?

Lucy *sits down at her table and spreads out the first of the papers on top of the confusion.*

Lesley (*into the telephone*)   129,769,500. 160,391,504.
227,489,864 . . . All right . . . ? Not at all. (*She puts the telephone down.*)

Lucy   Work-to-Rule Brings Chaos to Midlands. Storm of Protests over PM on TV . . . God, I hate this job. I hate this place.

Lesley   Would you be happier working at my table?

Lucy   No.

Lesley   I'm only discarding. I can work on top of the filing cabinets.

Lucy   Don't you hate it?

Lesley   Come on, you sit here.

Lucy   I don't want to sit there. Don't you hate this work?

Lesley   Yes.

Lucy   No, you don't. You love it.

Lesley   I'm dependent on it. That's what I hate.

Lucy   You're a natural for it. You've got an instinct for order.

Lesley   It's a compulsion. I hate the feeling of being compelled.

Lucy   You're as happy as a child making mud pies.

Lesley   I hate the mud.

Lucy   Mud pies are an improvement on mud.

Lesley   Mud pies are mud. And mud's mud.

Silence.

Lucy (*cutting*)   Middle East Dominates Ottawa Talks. Second Congo Fears Sway UN Vote . . . Mud, mud, glorious mud! Nothing quite like it for cooling the blood . . .

Lesley   You did think we should discard everything in the old Balance of Payments folders except the raw monthly figures, didn't you?

Lucy   *I* thought so?

Lesley   I *think* you did.

Lucy   *You* thought so.

Lesley   I think we did talk about it.

Lucy   I think you wondered whether I thought it would be a good idea.

Lesley   I think you thought it would.

Lucy   I think I thought whatever you thought.

Pause.

Lesley   I don't want to do it if you don't think it's a good idea.

Lucy   No. (*She laughs.*)

Lesley   What?

Lucy   Yes! I do think it's a good idea!

Pause.

Lesley   Look, all I can do is to make suggestions. It's up to you to say whether you accept them or not.

Lucy   I do accept them. All of them. Sight unseen. Nuclear power stations. What are we filing them under these days?

Atomic Energy Authority, or Central Electricity Generating
Board?

Lesley   Nuclear power stations? We file them under Nuclear
Power Stations.

Lucy   Oh. Well, that's one way of doing it.

Lesley   Unless you'd like to go back to the old system?

Lucy   All right. We'll go back to the old system.

Lesley *looks at her.*

Lucy   I said we'll go back to the old system. Whatever that
was.

Lesley   Look, if you want to, you've only got to say.

Lucy   I've said.

Lesley   No, seriously.

Lucy   Seriously.

Pause.

Lesley   All right, we'll move the tables back together again.

Lucy   The tables?

Lesley   Isn't it the tables you're worrying about?

Lucy   I'm not worrying about anything.

Lesley   It *is* the tables, isn't it?

Lucy   No!

Lesley   It was just an idea, putting them round this way.

Lucy   It's a good idea.

Lesley   I thought you thought you'd be happier if your stuff
wasn't spreading over on to my table all the time.

Lucy   Is that what I thought?

Lesley   I *thought* that's what you thought.

Pause.

Lucy   I love looking at this bit of wall.

Lesley *jumps up and tries to move* **Lucy***'s table.* **Lucy** *holds on to it.*

Lucy   I like it! I like it, I like it, I like it!

Lesley *gives up.*

Lesley   It's this place that's getting us down. It'll be better when we've got things straight.

Lucy   *Haven't* we got things straight?

Lesley   We haven't finished getting them straight.

Lucy   You mean my table?

Lesley   Of course not.

Lucy   That'll be the day, though. When we've finished getting things straight. When we've got even my table straight.

Arnold *enters.* **Lucy** *clears a space on her table for him to spread his papers out on, then continues to work.*

Lesley   Are you still on fish today?

Arnold   Yes.

She goes to the filing cabinets.

Lesley   What did you have? You had Fish General, Fish EFTA, Fish EEC, Fish Iceland and Fish Norway.

Arnold   Did I?

Lesley (*getting the folders out*)   How's Megan?

Arnold   Fine.

Lesley   Is she managing the new leg all right?

Arnold   Yes.

Lesley   I was afraid she might have some difficulty when she moved off the temporary leg. But she's managing, is she?

Arnold   Do fish sleep at night?

Geoffrey *enters, carrying a dispatch case full of wrapped magazines.*

Geoffrey   Here you are. This is what you've been waiting for. Fresh this morning – picked them myself. These'll bring the roses back to your cheeks. Oh Gawd, it's Arnold! The old maestro himself!

Lesley   In the in-basket, please.

Geoffrey   In the in-basket they shall go. In the in and out the out. How's Arnold today?

Arnold   Fine.

Geoffrey   And how's Megan?

Arnold   Fine.

Geoffrey   On the mend?

Arnold   Yes.

Geoffrey   That's right. Home soon. Before you know where you are you'll be wishing she was still in hospital. Because we all know the kind of thing you get up to while her back's turned. Don't we, Lesley?

Lesley *smiles obligingly.*

Geoffrey   Don't we, Lucy? I say we all know the kind of thing Arnold gets up to while his old lady's out of the way.

Lucy   Do we?

Geoffrey   'Do we?' she says. Oh dear. What's got into her today?

Lesley (*giving* **Arnold** *the folders*)   Fish General, Fish EFTA, Fish EEC, Fish Iceland, Fish Norway.

Geoffrey   Still on the fish? I thought you'd be on to the meat by now.

Lesley (*giving* **Arnold** *another folder*)   I thought you might be interested in some of this stuff on the Chilean fishery limits as background. And there's quite a good article in this issue of *Nature* about changing patterns of fish distribution.

Arnold   Oh.

Geoffrey 'Oh', he says.

Arnold *balances the stuff that* **Lesley** *has given him on top of everything else on* **Lucy***'s desk.*

Lesley   Didn't we decide you'd be happier working at this table?

She pulls out a chair at the third table, and waits by it firmly.

Arnold   Oh.

Geoffrey 'Oh,' he says. 'I like sitting at Lucy's table.'

Arnold *looks slowly back and forth between the two tables. Finally he decides to gather up his stuff and move to the new table.*

Geoffrey   But off he goes. Good as gold.

Lesley   You can work here without being disturbed.

Geoffrey   Look at him, tucked away up there.

Lesley   And I've written down the number of the Transport and General Office in Hull.

She hands him a piece of paper. **Arnold** *gazes at it.*

Lesley   You know there are problems about the unionisation of the trawlermen?

Arnold   Are there?

Lesley   You probably ought to have a word with them about it, oughtn't you?

Geoffrey 'Phone someone up?' he says. 'That's certainly not what I'd got in mind!'

Arnold *goes to the telephone on* **Lesley***'s table and picks up the receiver.*

Geoffrey   Well, would you believe it?

Lesley   Wouldn't you be happier using the phones in the News Room?

Geoffrey   The News Room? Oh dear. That takes a bit of thinking about. He didn't know there *were* any phones in the News Room.

Arnold *puts the receiver down and goes towards the door.*

Geoffrey   Oh Gawd! You've got to hand it to her, you know. She's certainly got this one trained.

Arnold *stops.*

Geoffrey   No, he's stopped.

Arnold *goes back to the third table, and collects up all his folders and papers.*

Geoffrey   What's this? Change of plan.

Arnold *goes towards the door.*

Geoffrey   Oh dear. He's packed his bags. You've scared him off altogether.

Lesley *(calling)*   Sorry! You won't forget to sign for the folders?

Arnold   Oh. *(He signs.)*

Geoffrey   Cheer up, Arnold! They always get you in the end. That's what women are for. Bless their little cotton socks.

Arnold *goes out.*

Geoffrey   Poor old Arnold. Doesn't know what's hit him. Does he, Lucy?

Lucy   Doesn't he?

Geoffrey   You're very quiet these days. Hiding away in your little corner down here. *(To **Lesley**.)* A terrible trial she used to be to all of us! Do you remember that? Or was that before your time?

Lesley   I wouldn't say she'd changed.

Geoffrey   Uproar there used to be in here! People carrying on! Everything everywhere! Isn't that right, Lucy?

Lucy   Yes.

Geoffrey   Yes. She agrees. She's with me. But she's a reformed character now. *(To **Lucy**.)* What's come over you?

Lucy   Do shut up, Geoffrey.

Geoffrey   No, it's funny, though, isn't it? Because you've got a nice little playmate in here now. Which is what you always wanted.

Lesley   Well, I suppose we must be getting on with our work.

Geoffrey   That's right, Lesley, you get on with your work.

Lucy   What she means, Geoffrey, is hop it.

Geoffrey   I know what she means! (*To* **Lesley**.) No, seriously, I remember her sitting here in despair saying, 'I'll never get this place straight!' Tears streaming down her face. Isn't that right, Lucy? Tears streaming down your face? And now you've got it straight, and everything in the garden's lovely, and you've sat yourself down in the corner here and gone into a decline.

Lesley   Next thing we know the tea trolley will be round.

Geoffrey   No, seriously – I'm being serious now – I've seen this happen over and over again. People get what they've always wanted, and what they've always wanted turns out to be not what they want at all. Take old Arnold. He and his good lady don't get along. Right?

Lucy   Geoffrey . . .

Geoffrey   No, we all know this. Lesley knows this. It's no secret.

Lucy   If we all know it we don't need to hear it again.

Geoffrey   No, listen! I'm making a serious point. All Arnold needed to make him happy was to see the back of his good lady. So what happens? His good lady obligingly goes off to hospital, poor girl, bless her heart, and leaves Arnold on his own. And is old Arnold then the bachelor gay, out on the town every night and chasing all the girls? No, he's not. He's still as miserable as sin. He still creeps off home at nine o'clock every night looking as if he's surrendering to his bail. Aren't I right, Lucy? You've seen him.

Lucy *works on in silence.*

Geoffrey   Silence reigned and they all got wet. (*To* **Lesley**.) What's the matter with her these days . . . ?

Lesley *shakes her head and frowns.*

Geoffrey   Now *she's* shaking her head at me . . . ! (*Realises.*) Oh dear. Have I put my foot in it?

Lucy   Yes.

Geoffrey   Oh dear oh dear. Sorry about that, Lucy. I didn't realise.

Lucy   Nothing much to realise.

Geoffrey   Arnold's billeted on you, then, while Megan's away? Oh, well, no wonder he's still looking miserable. (*To* **Lesley**.) I said no wonder he's still looking miserable, if old Lucy's keeping him on the straight and narrow.

Lesley *smiles obligingly.*

Geoffrey   Oh dear me, though. I walked right into that one, didn't I?

Lucy   Wallop.

Geoffrey   Well, well, well.

Lucy   I thought you knew everything.

Geoffrey   I thought I knew most things that go on round here.

Lucy   You're losing your grip.

Geoffrey   No, it's true, Lucy. I'm getting on. I'm getting old. Another couple of years and you'll be taking the list round for me.

Lucy   More than a couple of years, Geoffrey.

Geoffrey   No. Year after next.

Lucy   Year after next? It can't be!

Geoffrey   It can be. It is. Then what, Lucy? Then what?

Lucy   You'll have the time of your life.

Geoffrey   What, no evenings to take round? No galleys, no page proofs? No Lucy to talk to?

Lucy   Bit of peace and quiet at last.

Geoffrey   That's what we all want – a bit of peace and quiet. The only thing we don't want is a lot of peace and quiet. Oh well. Mustn't think about it. I'll be all right. Sorry about my little clanger.

Lucy   No. Quite funny, really. (*She laughs.*)

Geoffrey   She's off! She's happy again!

Lucy   What about you?

Geoffrey   When am I ever not?

Lucy   Our usual merry selves.

Geoffrey   As long as we can go on laughing we'll be all right.

Lucy   We'll be all right.

Geoffrey (*squeezing her shoulder emotionally*)   You'll be all right, Lucy, love, whatever happens.

He goes out.

Lesley   Sorry. I didn't manage that very well.

Lucy   No need to manage anything on *my* behalf, sugar.

Silence.

Lesley   Lucy, when Megan comes back from hospital . . . Arnold is going to move out? He is going to go home?

Lucy   You're worried about Megan?

Lesley   I've never met Megan.

Lucy   Well, don't worry about Arnold. I get him out of the George by nine every night. I get him to the hospital three times a week. What more do you want?

Lesley   I don't mean Arnold. You've been smashing about him. I mean . . . *you.*

Lucy   Oh. Me.

Lesley   You can't go on looking after him.

Lucy   Why not?

Lesley   Well, it's obvious why not!

Lucy   Look, Arnold's all right. He's worth more than most of the people in this office put together.

Lesley   But that's not the point, is it?

Lucy   What is the point?

Lesley   The point is that . . . well, you've got your life to lead, and you and Arnold . . . I mean, you're not actually *together*, are you.

Lucy *laughs.*

Lesley   Well, you aren't. Are you? It's not actually a *relationship*. Is it?

Lucy   I see why you wanted these chairs back to back.

Lesley   Anyway, he will be going? That's all I'm saying. When Megan comes home?

Lucy   Who says Megan's coming home?

Lesley   She's *not* coming home?

Lucy   Not just yet.

Lesley   I thought she was getting better . . . ? *Isn't* she getting better . . . ? You mean . . . she's never coming home?

Lucy   What do *you* think?

Lesley   Oh God.

Lucy   Yes. Poor old Megan.

Lesley   I wasn't thinking about Megan.

Lucy   I don't think about her much, either. It doesn't really bear thinking about.

Lesley   I was thinking more about you.

Lucy I wish you'd stop thinking about me.

Lesley I can't help it. Because in a way I feel responsible.

Lucy Policy decision: are we going to open a new folder for this Indian thing?

Lesley It wouldn't have happened if I hadn't arrived.

Lucy Four hundred dead. Four hundred aren't worth a brand-new buff folder all to themselves, are they?

Lesley If I hadn't arrived, you and John would still have been together.

Lucy John and I had split up long before you arrived.

Lesley You were living together!

Lucy Not then.

Lesley It was almost the first thing you told me when I got here.

Lucy Really? I can't remember the sequence of events now.

Lesley So I can't help feeling responsible.

Lucy Oh, do stop being responsible for everything! Allow other people a little responsibility for themselves! There are some things in the world that happen independently of you!

Silence.

Sorry. I know you want to make things better.

Lesley What I meant to happen, when I started this business with John, was for you to be forced to make up your mind about Wally.

Lucy *laughs.*

Lesley Well, that was one of the things I had in mind.

Lucy Lesley, you're a terrible person! Do you realise that? You're driving me mad! I'm going crazy, cooped up in here with you!

Lesley   I'm sorry.

Lucy   No, it was a kind thought.

Lesley   It wasn't supposed to be a kindness. I just wanted to get things straight.

Pause.

John and I are thinking of getting married.

Lucy *laughs.* **Lesley** *waits.*

Lucy (*stops laughing.*)   Sorry. I mean, congratulations. (*She laughs.*)

Lesley   It's not for *my* benefit. I wouldn't normally have suggested marriage.

Lucy   Wouldn't you? Normally?

Lesley   I mean, not in normal circumstances. Not in any other circumstances.

Lucy   But John being John . . .

Lesley   Well, that's the point. I think he needs a fairly definite framework to his life. He does tend to go off in different directions.

Lucy   He does, yes.

Lesley   I can't help feeling he'd benefit from being rather more pinned down.

Lucy   I think pinning down is exactly what he needs. Preferably without anaesthetics.

John *enters. He drapes himself over a filing cabinet.* **Lesley** *doesn't look at him. She works.* **Lucy** *looks at him with interest and amusement.*

John   What proportion of our total energy output is spent not upon production but upon . . . I don't know exactly how to put this . . . but as it were the *rearrangement* of the world's contents? Transportation of goods and people, transmission of information by television, et cetera, et cetera. Rearrangement of information by computer, et cetera, et cetera . . . and this

I should say is for a supplement on the communications industry . . .

Lesley *goes to the filing cabinets and searches.*

John   . . . though I suppose, when one comes to think about it, production as well has to be seen as a form of rearrangement . . .

Lucy   Congratulations.

John   Well, I don't suppose it's an entirely original thought.

Lucy   On your engagement.

John   Sorry?

Lesley   I told her we were thinking of getting married.

John   Oh. Yes, well, it's still as it were at the committee stage.

Lucy   You've proposed, and so on?

John   I've put in an outline proposal.

Lucy   An outline proposal?

John   As one might say.

Lucy   And you've received – as one might say – provisional planning approval?

John   As it were.

Lucy   An as it were engagement?

John   As we call it in the trade.

Lucy   Well, as it were congratulations.

John   That's all right.

Lucy   That's all right? What do you mean, 'That's all right'?

John   *Isn't* it all right?

Lucy   For God's sake, John! When somebody says 'Congratulations' you don't say 'That's all right'!

John   No, I suppose you don't. (*He laughs.*)

Lesley (*putting a folder in front of him*)   This is a breakdown of energy uses which includes transport . . .

John   What do I mean? I mean, if that's all right with you.

Lucy   You mean, 'Cheers.'

John   I mean, 'The same to you.'

Lucy   You mean, 'Sit down, sit down, this one's on me.'

Lucy and **John** *laugh foolishly.* **Lesley** *goes out.* **Lucy** *stops laughing.*

Lucy   Oh dear. Perhaps you ought to run after her.

John   I probably ought.

Lucy   Sorry.

John   Not your fault.

Lucy   I shouldn't have joked about it.

John   She's no sense of humour. That's where it went wrong.

Lucy   I shouldn't say that.

John   Not a flicker.

Lucy   No . . . Won't that be a bit tricky?

John   Disastrous, I should think. (*He starts to laugh again.*)

Lucy   John! You are serious about this thing? You're not, are you?

John   Of course I am! Or rather . . . Well . . . *I* don't know . . .

Lucy   You *are* a rat.

John   There's nothing I can do about it! It's my fate! It's what was to be! Antecedent truth – always rather a puzzle for philosophers.

Lucy   You are, you know – you're a rat.

John   No, that's my conception of life at the moment. A process of slowly as it were falling off a cliff. Catching on branches and ricocheting off ledges on the way. I quite like the sensation.

Lucy   On second thoughts you're not even a rat. You're just a great perambulating heap of blancmange.

John   There are some people who like blancmange.

Lucy   Not Lesley.

John   No, not Lesley. Well, yes, Lesley. She likes digging it around with her spoon. She keeps saying she thinks our relationship ought to be more as it were *defined*. So we sit there by the hour and as it were *define* it.

Lucy   While you slip further and further down in the chair.

John   Getting less and less defined.

Lucy   Like a blancmange melting.

They catch each other's eye and laugh.

John   Anyway, let's slide off tonight and talk about it all over a plate of nostalgic prawn biryani.

Lucy   What?

John   What?

Lucy   I must say!

John   Must say what?

Lucy   You're supposed to be engaged!

John   Yes, but we can meet in the George. She never goes in there.

Lucy   Don't be daft.

John   Look, all I'm proposing is a prawn biryani.

Lucy   I know your prawn biryanis.

John   Nine o'clock in the George.

Lucy   What about Arnold, just for a start?

John   What about Arnold?

Lucy   Arnold doesn't like prawn biryani.

John   Arnold won't be eating prawn biryani. Arnold isn't as one might say invited.

Lucy   Then I've got to get his supper, haven't I?

John   Arnold can get his own supper for once.

Lucy   You know what'll happen if I leave Arnold on his own for the evening.

John   We'll get someone to babysit.

Lucy   Anyway, never mind Arnold.

John   I'm not minding Arnold.

Lucy   Arnold's got nothing to do with it.

John   It was you who brought Arnold up.

Nora *enters.*

Lucy   Only to show you the whole idea's too silly even to talk about.

Nora   Lucy . . . Hello, John . . . Not intruding, am I?

Lucy   No, no.

Nora   A little bird has been whispering in my ear . . .

Lucy   What little bird? Which little bird?

Nora   Never you mind. But I think the time has come to get a few things straightened out.

John   Well, I'll be sliding along.

Nora   No, this concerns you, too, John.

Lucy   What is all this?

Nora   Lucy, you've been a real brick ever since Megan went into hospital. I know what you've done for Arnold, and you needn't think I don't. But I knew it would be too much for you. I said so right at the beginning. Didn't I, John? I knew she couldn't do a full-time job running this library, and look after you, and keep dear old Arnold on the straight and narrow. She's had a jolly good try, and we're all very proud of her. You've *both* been real bricks. I didn't realise what a kind-hearted old thing you were.

John   Me?

Nora   Having Arnold round there with you every night.

John   With *me?*

Nora   Don't be silly, John. We're all grown up here. We all know about you and Lucy.

John   Oh. I see. Well . . .

Nora   It's exactly the same for you as for any other young couple. You've got your own life to lead. You can't look after someone else's grandad as well. It's different for me, because since Freddie died I've been all on my ownsome, and there's nothing easier for me than to buy an extra chop and peel a few more spuds. In fact it'll do me a lot of good to make the effort again.

Lucy   Nora, it's very kind of you, but he won't come, you know.

Nora   You leave him to me. All he needs is a bit of firmness. He's been indulged for too long. Don't forget I've brought up a husband and two children. They may pull sulky faces and say, 'Don't want to. Not going to.' But secretly they're jolly pleased to be told what to do and when to do it.

Lucy   John, say something.

John   What? Oh. Thanks.

Lucy   Oh, for God's sake.

Nora   That's right, John. You two go out and enjoy yourselves for once.

John   Yes, we *were* thinking of sliding off for a plate of something.

Nora   And don't you worry about Arnold. I'll come and collect him as soon as he finishes, and feed him, and drive him home afterwards.

Lesley *enters.*

Nora   Lesley, love . . .

Lesley (*to* **Nora**)   He's in the News Room. He's on the phone still.

The telephone rings.

I'll get it. (*Into the telephone.*) Library . . .

Nora   No, we'll talk him round one way or another, never you fear. And if we can't talk him round we'll jolly well *drag* him round.

Lucy   This is you and the little bird, is it?

Nora   And a sweet, kind little bird it is, who likes to put things right in the world.

Lesley (*into the telephone*)   You know that there were also three charges of demanding money with menaces . . . ? Hold on.

She goes to the filing cabinets and searches. **Lucy** *begins to laugh to herself.*

Nora   I don't know what's so funny about that . . . What's the joke? John, do you know what the joke is?

John   Yes.

Nora   But if it means that you two are free to go out for a meal together . . .

Lucy *laughs.*

Lesley (*into the telephone*)   Hello . . . ? No, Stevens was the one the judge said was the artist in evil, who would stop at nothing to further his dastardly aims. O'Connor was merely the pathetic victim of his own ignorance and childish greed. All right? (*She puts the telephone down. To* **Nora**.) I'll see if he's off the phone . . .

She goes out.

Lucy   And off she flutters.

John   To give Arnold a smart peck on the bum.

Lucy (*laughs*)   I'm sorry.

John   Cheep cheep!

Lucy   It's not funny!

Nora   It's not at all funny.

John   It's tragic irony. (*He starts to laugh.*)

Nora   I think it *is* rather tragic that you don't appreciate her thoughtfuless.

Lucy   It is! It's heartbreaking!

John   We're rats! We're what one observer has termed 'perambulating heaps of blancmange'.

Nora   I really don't understand you two.

John   You're not the only one. We don't understand ourselves.

Wally *enters.*

Nora   Oh dear, and here's Wally with more jokes.

Wally (*ignores them all, stunned*)   Well, it's happened.

Nora   No funny turns today, Wally.

Wally   It's finally happened.

Nora   Wally! They've got the giggles already.

Wally   You won't laugh when I tell you.

Nora   Oh yes they will.

Wally *watches them gloomily.*

Lucy (*controls herself*)   Hello, Wally. Don't take any notice of us.

Wally *waits for them to recover completely.*

John   I love his timing.

Lucy   I hope you've really got that horse outside today. It's now or never.

John   Perfect deadpan.

Wally *waits. The laughter suddenly dries up.*

Lucy   What is it?

Nora   What's happened?

Lucy   What is it, Wally?

Wally   We've folded.

They gaze at him.

We've ceased publication. I ran into Tom Arthur on the stairs. He'd just come out of the Chairman's office. Tom looked as if he didn't know what had hit him.

Pause.

Nora   But we couldn't simply . . . *stop*!

Wally   We've stopped.

Nora   But they couldn't just . . .

Wally   We're not producing a paper tonight!

Nora   But . . . the unions . . .

Wally   The what?

Nora   The unions.

Wally   What about the unions?

Nora   The unions wouldn't stand for it.

Wally   It's too late, Nora! It's all over.

Silence. The telephone rings.

Nora   Well, I'm sorry, but I don't believe it. I just don't believe it. Do you, John?

John *shrugs.*

Nora   Do you, Lucy?

Lucy *crosses to* **Lesley**'s *table and answers the telephone.*

Lucy   Library . . . Charles . . . Yes, we've just heard. Wally's here . . . I know – we can't, either . . . We're just sitting here stunned . . . Thanks, anyway . . . (*She puts the telephone down.*) Charles Harland.

John   Well, we all saw it coming.

Nora   But not yet! Not like this!

John   Whoever saw anything coming yet, or like this?

Wally   You feel as if the ground's opened up beneath you.

Nora   We're not going to take this lying down, are we?

John   What can we do?

Nora   There must be something!

John   There's nothing, Nora.

Nora   Surely we can protest . . . ?

Wally   Oh, we can protest.

Lucy   We can put in a really strong protest.

John   Then we can argue about the compensation.

Wally   Poor old Tom looked as if he didn't know whether he was on his head or his heels.

Geoffrey *enters with the evening papers.*

Geoffrey   Here you are! Read all about it! And a terrible state the world's in today. Plane crash in the Pacific. Motorway Madness Hits City Centre. Fares going up. Bad news all round – nothing like it for putting the sparkle back in your eye!

He puts the papers on **Lucy**'s *table.*

Geoffrey   Hello, Wally! What's *your* trouble, then? End of the world? (*To* **Lucy**.) What's *his* trouble . . . ? (*He takes in all their expressions.*) Bad news?

Lucy   Bad news.

Nora   It's the paper, Geoffrey.

John   We've folded.

Nora   Wally met Tom Arthur on the stairs.

Lucy   He'd just come out of the Chairman's office.

Geoffrey *sits down.*

John   We all saw this coming.

Wally   Tom was as white as a sheet.

Silence. The telephone rings.

Lucy (*into the telephone*)   Library . . . No, we can't, either . . .
Isn't it? . . . We're just sitting here saying the same thing . . .
Nothing at all, is there? We can't think of anything . . . Protest
– yes, that's what we thought . . . If we do have any ideas I'll
call you back . . . (*She puts the telephone down.*) I think everyone's
just . . . stunned.

Geoffrey (*hiding his eyes from them*)   It's been going for over a
hundred years, this paper.

John   Well, it's just another development site now.

Geoffrey   Two world wars. Three kings. Two queens.

John   Just building rubble, a few second-hand desks, a few
second-hand typewriters.

Nora   A few second-hand people.

Geoffrey   It's all right for me. I'm an old man.

Nora   I certainly shan't find another job, at my age.

Wally   We're none of us going to find jobs in this town.

Nora (*to* **Wally**)   It's people like you I feel sorriest for, with
families to support.

Wally   What about Lucy?

Lucy   Oh, it doesn't matter about me.

Geoffrey   You know who I feel sorriest for? You may think this is ridiculous, but I feel sorriest for little Lesley. She hasn't been here long, I know. But she's put her whole heart and soul into this place.

Lucy   Got the whole thing reorganised.

John   And now it's just so much waste paper.

Wally   There are some real swine around in this world.

Nora   There are, Wally, there certainly are.

John   And we all know who they are round here.

Geoffrey   What do they care about someone like Lesley?

Lucy   They don't even know she exists.

Geoffrey   This is only her second job, and she gave it everything she's got.

Lucy   Another week and she'd have got this whole place up to date.

Geoffrey   Slaving away, she was, to get all the dead wood out of it.

John   Well, it's all dead now. (*He picks up one of the folders which* **Lesley** *got out.*) Balance of Payments 1957–61. (*He opens it and looks through the cuttings.*) Oh God, look at it all!

Lucy *ceremoniously sweeps all the cuttings out of the folder on to the floor.*

Nora   I shouldn't throw them on the floor, Lucy. Someone will only have to pick them up.

Lucy   Why? They can just stay there now.

John (*picking up another folder*)   Balance of Payments 1961–64.

Lucy *sweeps all the cuttings out of it.*

Nora   But, Lucy, someone might want those cuttings one day.

Lucy   I don't think so, Nora.

Geoffrey   Dead leaves, Nora. Dead leaves.

John (*picking up another folder*)   Balance of Payments 1964–66.

Lucy (*sweeping the cuttings out of the folder*)   That's what we've been collecting all these years! Waste paper!

She pulls open drawers at random.

Look at it! Biology, Broadcasting . . . Commodities, Communities . . . Fascism, Fashion . . . That's my life in there! Cyclamates. (*She takes the folder out.*) Remember Cyclamates?

John   Defoliants!

Lucy   Fly away Cyclamates! (*She throws the cuttings into the air.*)

John   Fly away Defoliants! (*He does likewise.*)

Geoffrey   That's the spirit!

Wally (*looking in one of the drawers*)   Look at all this stuff! (*He takes out a folder.*) Weedkiller . . .

Lucy   Cryogenics! (*She scatters it.*) Go on, Wally.

Wally   Shall I chuck it!

John   Ecology! (*He scatters it.*) Chuck it, Wally!

Geoffrey   Up in the air, Wally!

Wally (*scattering his folder*)   There she blows!

Lucy   Hurrah!

Wally   That's good! I like that!

Geoffrey   Here, let me get my hands on this!

John   Elections General!

Lucy   Censorship!

John   Up with Censorship!

Lucy   Up it goes!

Wally   War!

John   Up with War!

Geoffrey   What's this? Plutonium! Oh, it gets it off your chest, doesn't it.

Wally   Come on, Nora! Here's one for you! Women!

Nora   I'm too old for this sort of thing.

Geoffrey   Get stuck in, Nora! No messing about!

Lucy   Let your hair down, Nora!

John   Let rip, Nora!

Nora   Oh dear . . . Up with Women!

Geoffrey   That's the way!

Wally   Yoga!

John   Electricity! Electronics!

Lucy   Dentists! Dyslexia!

Geoffrey   Poetry!

Nora   Zinc!

The telephone rings.

John   Embassies! Embroidery!

Lucy (*into the telephone*)   Library . . .

Wally   Libraries!

Lucy (*into the telephone*)   Or what was the Library . . .

Geoffrey   Radiation!

Nora   Zoos!

Lucy (*into the telephone*)   What . . . ? Can't hear . . .

John   Enzymes! Environment!

Lucy (*into the telephone*)   Oh, drop dead. (*She puts the telephone down.*)

John   The European Economic Community! God, that was beautiful.

Wally (*singing*)   Over my shoulder goes Vietnam!

Geoffrey   Over my shoulder goes Sex!

Nora   Vandalism! I must say, this is rather fun!

Lucy (*climbing on to the filing cabinets*)   And now here is a Party Political Broadcast on behalf of the Conservative and Unionist Party. (*She scatters the contents of the folder.*)

Arnold *enters.*

Lucy   Arnold! Come in!

Nora   Just the man we want to see!

Arnold   Something about grub at your place tonight?

Nora   That's right! Grub at my place!

Lucy   I can see I shall have to eat my words. (*She chews cuttings.*)

Arnold (*noticing the state of the room*)   Oh . . .

Geoffrey   He's noticed!

John   European Parliament!

Nora   Come and join the fun, Arnold!

She takes him by the arm and draws him across to the filing cabinets.

Geoffrey   Pitch in, Arnold!

Wally   Here you are. Grab a handful of Violence!

Arnold   But what . . . ?

Nora   The paper's folded!

John   You're on the street, Arnold! Euthanasia!

Lucy   We're all on the street! Here – chuck this. Computers!

Arnold *gazes at the folder* **Lucy** *has given him.*

Geoffrey   We've gone bust!

Lucy   We've broken up!

Wally   It's the summer holidays!

Nora   It's Christmas!

Lucy   It's snowing!

John   It's blossom time!

Wally   Chuck it, Arnold!

Arnold   Folded? The paper?

Geoffrey   Kaput!

John   Down the tubes!

Geoffrey   So we're having a party to celebrate!

John   We're having an orgy!

Lucy   We're having a white wedding!

She sprinkles cuttings over **Arnold** *and* **Nora**.

Lucy (*singing*)   Here comes the bride . . . !

Geoffrey, **Wally** *and* **John** *take up the anthem and scatter cuttings over the happy couple.*

Nora   They're marrying us off, Arnold! Well, I must kiss the bridegroom!

She kisses the still bewildered **Arnold**.

Geoffrey   I'm the bride's father!

He kisses **Nora**.

Wally (*climbing on to the filing cabinets*)   I'm the best man! I have to kiss the bridesmaid!

He kisses **Lucy**.

John (*climbing on to the filing cabinets*)   I'm the vicar! I have to kiss everyone!

He kisses **Lucy** *and* **Wally**.

Wally   Buzz off, John! This is serious.

John   But I'm the vicar!

Wally   Shove off!

John   I can't have this sort of thing going on in my church unless I'm allowed to join in!

Wally   Get out of it, get out of it!

He hits **John** *with the folder he is holding. It disintegrates.*

Geoffrey   Seconds out! Bing bing!

John   I'm as one might say shelling you!

He throws a loaded folder at **Wally**.

Wally   Now, watch it, Professor!

John   Woomph! (*He hurls another folder.*)

Wally   Right, this is war!

He grabs a folder out of a drawer and hurls it at **John**.

Geoffrey   Let's get the Prof!

He starts throwing folders at **John**.

Wally   All Souls, was it? Or All Fools?

Nora   Up Cambridge!

She bombards **John**.

Geoffrey   We're after you, Prof!

John   What is this?

He jumps from filing cabinet to filing cabinet, trying to avoid the missiles, most of which in any case disintegrate in mid-air like shrapnel shells.

Missed! You bastards! What *is* all this?

Nora   It's that voice of yours, John!

Geoffrey   That la-di-da voice!

Wally   It's your bloody awful leaders!

John   My leaders?

Wally   It was your leaders that finished this paper off!

John   What finished this paper off, if you want to know . . .

Geoffrey   Here – a load of Soya Beans!

John   Oh, pack it up!

Geoffrey   Temper, temper!

John   What finished this paper off . . .

Nora   Unidentified Flying Objects!

John   I'm trying to make a serious point!

Lucy (*sprinkling cuttings on her own*)   There's pansies, that's for thoughts . . .

Lesley *enters. Stops. Stares.*

John   What killed this paper was –

Wally   Caviar!

John   – was being dead already!

Nora   No, John, I won't have that!

Wally   Bicycles!

Nora   It was a fine paper, and let's never forget that!

Geoffrey   It was a great paper!

Nora   It was the best!

John   It was just a mouldering heap of waste paper!

Wally   Au Pair Girls!

Nora   What about the people on it? You're not trying to tell us there was another team anywhere half as good as this one?

John   What, *us*?

Nora   Yes, *us*!

John   Look at us! Look at us! We're *jokes*!

Wally   Disasters Natural!

John   And as for *you*, you pathetic . . . fiddle-faddler . . . !

He seizes a heavy volume and turns on **Wally** *with real savagery.*

Wally   Dishwashers!

John   Right! That's it! I'm going to break your bloody skull in . . . ! (*He sees* **Lesley**, *and stops.*) What?

Nora   Oh, hello, Lesley.

Wally, **Geoffrey** *and* **Arnold** *turn to look at her.*

Geoffrey   Come on, Lesley!

Nora   Party time!

Wally   Come and throw Butter and Butterflies at John!

Geoffrey   We were just talking about you, Lesley. We were just saying what a shame it was. Weren't we, Nora?

Nora   How hard you'd worked to get this place straight.

Geoffrey   How you'd really put your heart and soul into it.

John   And now look at it!

Lesley *looks.*

Lucy   There's rue for you. (*She scatters a handful of cuttings.*) There's Twenty Mile Oil Slick Hits South Coast.

Silence.

Wally   She doesn't understand.

Nora   She doesn't know what's happened.

Wally   The paper's folded, Lesley!

Geoffrey   We've gone bust!

Lesley   So I gather.

Geoffrey   She does know.

Wally   We're just killing John to celebrate. We're going to set fire to all this lot. Then we're going to stick John on a window pole and barbecue him. Will you have a slice?

Geoffrey   Acupuncture! (*He scatters it.*)

Nora   She can't take it in, poor love!

Lucy   This is all scrap now!

John   The paper's closed!

Lesley   The management's closed it. But we shan't accept that, shall we?

Nora   Shan't accept it?

Lesley   We'll take it over! Won't we? We'll run it ourselves!

Silence.

Isn't that what you've been talking about? Everyone in the composing room is a hundred per cent. I said I thought we'd be, too.

Geoffrey   We couldn't do that, Lesley.

Lesley   Why not?

John   Well, for about a million bloody reasons.

Geoffrey   There's all sorts of reasons, Lesley.

John   Who'd sell us newsprint, for a start?

Geoffrey   We don't know how to run a newspaper.

Lesley   I thought we could just carry on as normal. Bring out tomorrow's paper . . .

Nora   Oh, we could bring out tomorrow's paper.

Geoffrey   No problems about tomorrow's paper.

John   But then what happens?

Lesley   I thought we could think about that tomorrow. Couldn't we? Sorry.

Silence.

Lucy   I might have known Lesley wouldn't let us off as easily as that.

Wally   What's she saying?

Lucy   Thinks we should take the paper over. Run it ourselves.

Wally   Take the paper over?

Lucy   Don't look at me.

Wally   Run it ourselves?

Lucy   Not my idea.

Wally   Yes . . . Yes! Why not?

Arnold   The *People's Daily*! (*He laughs.*)

Nora   I suppose we could bring out tomorrow's paper . . .

Geoffrey   See how that went . . .

Arnold   The local *Pravda*!

John   We're not seriously thinking about this, are we?

Wally   We couldn't do any worse than the present lot.

Nora   We could certainly do better than them, John!

Geoffrey   We could knock spots off that gang!

Arnold   Put a rocket up their arse! (*He laughs.*)

Wally   There must be a market in this place for a really good local daily.

Geoffrey   Of course there must. They don't know how to run a paper.

Nora   You must accept that, John.

John   I suppose we could think about it.

Geoffrey   Think about it? Of course! We've got to think about it!

John   I think that's all I'm saying.

Lesley   We're meeting in the subs' room to discuss it.

Nora   What – now?

Lesley   Now, yes, now. So we can get the paper out tonight.

Nora   Come on, then!

Geoffrey   All for one, and one for all!

Wally   Where are we going?

Geoffrey   Meeting in the subs'.

They all make a move, then stop and look round at the wreckage.

Nora   Oh dear. Sorry about all this, Lesley.

Lesley   No, I'm sorry to have spoiled your fun.

Wally   This is terrible, though.

Geoffrey   We're going to need all this after all.

Nora   I knew we were wrong.

Geoffrey   Oh, I knew we were wrong all right.

Nora   Look at it!

Geoffrey   What have we done?

Lucy   Sorry, Lesley.

Lesley   Well . . . spilt milk.

Nora   We'll clear it up after the meeting.

Geoffrey   We'll all help. We'll all do our bit.

John
All the king's horses and all the king's men
Somehow put Humpty together again.

Lesley (*discreetly urging them out*)   Anyway, the subs', the subs' . . .

Nora   We're all going to have to be as good as gold now to make up.

Geoffrey   Back to earth with a bump. Still, it was fun while it lasted.

He goes out.

Nora   Arnold . . . You come and sit by me.

Arnold   Machine-gun the lot of them! (*He laughs.*)

Nora *and* **Arnold** *go out, followed by* **Lesley**.

Wally (*to* **John**)   Sorry about all that. I didn't mean what I said.

John   Of course not. Nothing means what it appears to mean.

Wally   I think your leaders are the only thing worth reading in the paper.

John   And I think your stuff is what we call in the business brilliant.

Wally   They *are* brilliant. Arnold, Nora, all of them.

John   Arnold and Nora, too.

Wally   Of course I am!

John (*to* **Lucy**)   So – nine o'clock? Biryani?

Lucy   Go on. Your fiancée's going to be wondering where you are.

John   My as it were fiancée. My, as I privately like to think of her, ex as it were fiancée.

Lucy   The paper today. You tomorrow.

Wally   Come on, madam. Are we eloping or aren't we?

John   We've got the staff, we've got the jokes. How can we fail?

He goes out.

Wally   We will, though, won't we? After we've taken the paper over?

Lucy   Wally . . . you could come back to my place this evening, if you like. No one else there. I'll get a bottle of wine. You could say you were late because of the meeting about the closure.

Wally (*smiling*)   First full moon.

Lucy   Now or never, Wally.

Wally   Sooner or later.

Lucy   Did you hear what I said?

Wally   When the horse is up to it.

Pause. **Lesley** *enters.*

Lesley   Oh – sorry.

Lucy   Go on, then, Wally. Go to the meeting.

Wally   One of these days. When the revolution comes.

Lucy   That *was* the revolution.

He squeezes her hand.

Wally   One of these days.

He goes out.

Lesley   You'd better come. We may want to talk about job cuts.

Lucy   You go. I'll get started in here . . .

She looks around at the chaos.

I'm sorry, Lesley! I'm so sorry!

Lesley   Your work as much as mine.

She picks up a few cuttings and puts them into a folder. **Lucy** *takes it out of her hands.*

Lucy   *I'll* do it . . . ! I'll work on this evening! I'll work all night!

She starts to pick up cuttings.

Lesley   I think they want me to chair this thing . . .

Lucy   Yes! Off you go! Chair the meeting! Save the paper!

She gets down on her hands and knees to work. **Lesley** *watches her for a moment, then goes out.*

Lucy (*sings to herself*)
A, B, C, D, E, F, G,
H, I, J, K, L, M, N . . .